Great Speeches

Edited by Sue Hackman

Hodder Education

A MEMBER OF HACHETTE LIVRE UK

Photo credits and acknowledgements can be found on p. 62.

Hachette's policy is to use papers that are natural, renewable and recyclable products and made from wood grown in sustainable forests. The logging and manufacturing processes are expected to conform to the environmental regulations of the country of origin.

Orders: please contact Bookpoint Ltd, 130 Milton Park, Abingdon, Oxon OX14 4SB. Telephone: (44) 01235 827720. Fax: (44) 01235 400454. Lines are open 9.00–5.00, Monday to Saturday, with a 24-hour message answering service. Visit our website at www.hoddereducation.co.uk

Impression number   5   4   3   2   1
Year   2012 2011 2010 2009 2008

Cover photo: Hulton Archive/Getty Images
Typeset in 12/14pt Bembo by Charon Tec Ltd (A Macmillan Company), Chennai, India
www.charontec.com

Printed in Great Britain by CPI Antony Rowe.

A catalogue record for this title is available from the British Library

ISBN 978 0340 966 334

Contents

War
Making the call to arms 25

Justice
Demanding rights 41

The American Dream
Speeches by Americans 53

Introduction

It is remarkable how a great speech can capture the ear, the heart and the mind. The speeches in this book were intended to be heard, of course, rather than to be read. And in many cases, the speakers also expected to be seen. What you have here are their speaking scripts. The speeches themselves were delivered in their voices, with their gestures and pauses. Some of them were shouted to huge crowds and others were spoken softly into a radio microphone. Speeches are closer to drama than any other art form, because they are meant to be performed.

It ought to be said that most great politicians had – and still do have – speechwriters who assembled ideas, and worked up concepts and phrases for them, until the speech 'worked'. Scores of people will have commented on the drafts, although quite a few of these speeches were scribbled out the night before.

It is obvious that a great speaker will choose the language that fits in their own mouth and suits their natural speaking style. If you listen closely, you can hear the speaker's voice in the speech. You may be able to track down tapes of the more recent speeches, so you can hear how they were delivered.

What makes a good speaker give a great speech? Certainly most of these speeches were made under pressure at an important moment in history or in the speaker's career. Yet there is something about them that goes beyond the time and place they were spoken, for they all touch on great themes such as justice, honour and the way life should be.

Many of the speeches were made when the speaker was in a tight spot and needed to justify, say, a war or an awkward decision. It is at such moments that a speaker will make enormous efforts to persuade their audience of the rightness of the cause, and appeal to their principles. This may be what lifts a speech from being just clever, or right, or well-written, to becoming a great and inspiring one.

Author note

It has been my privilege over the last few years to work with speechwriters and ministers on their speeches. On occasion I have had the thrill of hearing my own words and phrases come back to me through their mouths. I prepared this book whilst I was working for Alan Johnson, who was then Secretary of State for Education and Skills, and his speechwriter, the excellent Simon Lancaster. No-one could have more inspiring models of what it means to be honest in intention, brave in thought and respectful of the living language. I was reminded daily of the power of words to change people's lives. This book is dedicated to them.

Any speeches made by an American speaker have been transcribed in American English.

I Have a Dream

Visions of a better world

1

A fit country for heroes to live in

David Lloyd George was one of the greatest speakers of British politics. The war had just ended, and England was about to hold a general election when he made this speech describing what Britain should be like in peace time.

What is our task? To make Britain a fit country for heroes to live in. I am not using the word 'heroes' in any spirit of boastfulness, but in the spirit of humble recognition of the fact. I cannot think what these men have gone through. I have been there at the door of the furnace and witnessed it, but that is not being in it, and I saw them march into the furnace. There are millions of men who will come back. Let us make this land fit for such men to live in.

There is no time to lose. I want us to take advantage of this new spirit. Don't let us waste this victory merely in ringing joybells. Let us make victory the motive power to link the old land up in such measure that it will be nearer the sunshine than ever before, and that at any rate it will lift those who have been living in the dark places to a plateau where they will get the rays of the sun.

We cannot undertake that without a new Parliament. Those of you who have been at the front have seen the star shells*, how they light up the darkness and

★star shells: exploding flares which lit up the night sky

illuminate all the obscure places. The Great War has been like a gigantic star shell, flashing all over the land, illuminating the country and showing up the dark, deep places. We have seen places that we have never noticed before, and we mean to put these things right.

David Lloyd George, 1918

Prime Minister David Lloyd George gives a speech during World War I.

Postscript
David Lloyd George went on to win a landslide victory in the general election in the following month.

2

England is the country, and the country is England

Stanley Baldwin was born in the English countryside, and even as Prime Minister he often spoke about its special qualities. At the time of this speech, he had just regained his post after losing the vote in the previous year.

To me, England is the country, and the country is England. And when I ask myself what I mean by England, when I think of England when I am abroad, England comes to me through my various senses – through the ear, through the eye, and through certain imperishable scents. I will tell you what they are, and there may be those among you who feel as I do.

The sounds of England, the tinkle of the hammer on the anvil in the country smithy, the corncrake[1] on a dewy morning, the sound of the scythe against the whetstone, and the sight of a plough team coming over the brow of a hill, the sight that has been seen in England since England was a land, and may be seen in England long after the Empire has perished and every works in England has ceased to function, for centuries the one eternal sight of England.

The wild anemones in the woods in April, the last load at night of hay being drawn down a lane as the twilight comes on, when you can scarcely distinguish the figures of the horses as they take it home to the farm, and above all, most subtle, most penetrating and most moving, the smell of wood smoke coming up in an autumn evening, or the smell of the scotch fires[2]: that

---

[1] corncrake: a bird
[2] scotch fires: bonfires

wood smoke that our ancestors, tens of thousands of years ago, must have caught on the air when they were coming home with the results of the day's forage, when they were still nomads, and when they were still roaming the forests and plains of the continent of Europe.

These things strike down into the very depths of our nature, and touch chords that go back to the beginning of time and the human race, but they are chords that with every year of our life sound a deeper note in our innermost being.

Stanley Baldwin, 1924

Postscript
Stanley Baldwin remained Prime Minister until 1929 when he was voted out of office again. He became unpopular because he wished to keep peace with Hitler and the fascists. He died in 1947.

3

A world founded upon four essential human freedoms

Franklin D. Roosevelt was the President of the United States during World War II. In this speech, he is arguing to give help to Britain and the Allies. He appealed to people's sense of what was right.

In the future days, which we seek to make secure, we look forward to a world founded upon four essential human freedoms.

The first is freedom of speech and expression – everywhere in the world.

The second is freedom of every person to worship God in his own way – everywhere in the world.

The third is freedom from want – which, translated into world terms, means economic understandings which will secure to every nation a healthy peacetime life for its inhabitants – everywhere in the world.

The fourth is freedom from fear – which, translated into world terms, means a world-wide reduction of armaments to such a point and in such a thorough fashion that no nation will be in a position to commit an act of physical aggression against any neighbour – anywhere in the world.

Franklin D. Roosevelt, 1940

Postscript
The Americans gave financial help to Britain and joined the war themselves after the Japanese bombed Pearl Harbor in 1941.

4

I have a dream

This is probably the most famous speech ever made. Martin Luther King delivered it to a huge crowd in Washington. They had gathered to demand equal rights for black Americans.

We cannot turn back. There are those who are asking the devotees of civil rights, 'When will you be satisfied?' We can never be satisfied as long as the Negro is the victim of the unspeakable horrors of police brutality. We can never be satisfied as long as our bodies, heavy with the fatigue of travel, cannot gain lodging in the motels of the highways and the hotels of the cities. We cannot be satisfied as long as the Negro's basic mobility is from a smaller ghetto to a larger one. We can never be satisfied as long as a Negro in Mississippi cannot vote and a Negro in New York believes he has nothing for which to vote. No, no, we are not satisfied, and we will not be satisfied until justice rolls down like waters and righteousness like a mighty stream.

I am not unmindful that some of you have come here out of greater trials and tribulations. Some of you have come fresh from narrow jail cells. Some of you have come from areas where your quest for freedom left you battered by the storms of persecution and staggered by the winds of police brutality. You have been the veterans of creative suffering. Continue to work with the faith that unearned suffering is redemptive.

Go back to Mississippi, go back to Alabama, go back to South Carolina, go back to Georgia, go back to Louisiana, go back to the slums and ghettos of our northern cities, knowing that somehow this situation can and will be changed. Let us not wallow in the valley of despair.

I say to you today, my friends, that in spite of the difficulties and frustration of the moment I still have a dream. It is a dream deeply rooted in the American dream.

I have a dream that one day this nation will rise up and live out the true meaning of its creed: 'We hold these truths to be self-evident; that all men are created equal.'

I have a dream that one day on the red hills of Georgia the sons of former slaves and the sons of former slave-owners will be able to sit down together at the table of brotherhood.

I have a dream that one day even the state of Mississippi, a desert state sweltering with the heat of injustice and oppression, will be transformed into an oasis of freedom and justice.

Martin Luther King delivering his "I have a dream" speech in Washington, D.C.

I have a dream that my four little children will one day live in a nation where they will not be judged by the colour of their skin but by the content of their character.

I have a dream today.

I have a dream that one day the state of Alabama, whose governor's lips are presently dripping with the words of interposition and nullification, will be transformed into a situation where little black boys and black girls will be able to join hands with little white boys and white girls and walk together as sisters and brothers.

I have a dream today.

I have a dream that one day every valley shall be exalted, every hill and mountain shall be made low, the rough places will be made plains, and the crooked places will be made straight, and the glory of the Lord shall be revealed, and all flesh shall see it together.

This is our hope. This is the faith with which I return to the South. With this faith we will be able to hew out of the mountain of despair a stone of hope. With this faith we will be able to transform the jangling discords of our nation into a beautiful symphony of brotherhood. With this faith we will be able to work together, to pray together, to struggle together, to go to jail together, to stand up for freedom together, knowing that we will be free one day.

Martin Luther King, 1963

Postscript
Martin Luther King was assassinated in 1968, allegedly by James Earl Ray, but there are still conspiracy theories surrounding his death.

At a Moment Like This

Saying the right thing at the right moment

5

Cromwell dismisses Parliament

During the English Civil War, in which King Charles I had been executed, Oliver Cromwell led the country. Less enthusiastic members of Parliament were dismissed and the remaining 'rump' (the Rump Parliament) were lukewarm about Cromwell's reforms and slow to help. In the end, Cromwell lost his patience. In this famous speech he gives them a piece of his mind and sends them all home.

It is high time for me to put an end to your sitting in this place, which you have dishonoured by your contempt of all virtue, and defiled by your practice of every vice. Ye are a factious crew, and enemies to all good government; ye are a pack of mercenary wretches, and would like Esau to sell your country for a mess of potage[1], and like Judas betray your God for a few pieces of money[2]; is there a single virtue now remaining amongst you? Is there one vice you do not possess?

[1] like Esau to sell your country for a mess of potage: in the bible, Esau arrives home from hunting so tired and hungry that he buys a pot of stew from his twin brother Jacob, giving up in return everything he was due to inherit.

[2] like Judas betray your God for a few pieces of money: Judas, one of Jesus Christ's closest followers, told his enemies where they could find Jesus and arrest him. He was paid silver coins for his information. Jesus was arrested and condemned to death.

Ye have no more religion than my horse; gold is your God; which of you have not barter'd your conscience for bribes? Is there a man amongst you that has the least care for the good of the Commonwealth? Ye sordid prostitutes have you not defil'd this sacred place, and turn'd the Lord's temple into a den of thieves, by your immoral principles and wicked practices? Ye are grown intolerably odious to the whole nation; you were deputed here by the people to get grievances redress'd, are yourselves become the greatest grievance.

Your county therefore calls upon me to cleanse this Augean stable*, by putting a final period to your iniquitous proceedings in this House; and which by God's help, and the strength he has given me, I am now come to do; I command ye therefore, upon the peril of your lives, to depart immediately out of this place; go, get you out! Make haste! Ye venal slaves be gone! Go! Take away that shining bauble there, and lock up the doors. In the name of God, go!

Oliver Cromwell, 1653

Postscript

Cromwell put a new parliament in place, but this did no better. Within a year, he was made 'Lord Protector'. Many people thought that he had executed the King so he could become king himself. Two years after Cromwell died, Charles I's son (King

---

* **cleanse this Augean stable:** the legend of Hercules tells how he cleaned out the filthy stables of King Augeas by changing the course of a river to run through them.

Charles II) returned to England and the monarchy was restored in 1660.

6

Edward VIII abdicates the throne

King Edward VIII of England gave up the throne in 1936 to marry Mrs Wallace Simpson. She was an American woman who had been married before and her divorce had just come through. As king, Edward was the head of the Church of England and was forbidden to marry a divorcee. He had been king for less than a year when he made this broadcast from Windsor Castle.

At long last I am able to say a few words of my own. I have never wanted to withhold anything, but until now it has not been constitutionally possible for me to speak.

A few hours ago I discharged my last duty as King and Emperor, and now that I have been succeeded by my brother, the Duke of York, my first words must be to declare my allegiance to him. This I do with all my heart.

You all know the reasons which have impelled me to renounce the Throne. But I want you to understand that in making up my mind I did not forget the country or the Empire, which, as Prince of Wales, and lately as King, I have for twenty-five years tried to serve. But you must believe me when I tell you that I have found it impossible to carry the heavy burden of responsibility and to discharge my duties as King as I would wish to do without the help and support of the woman I love.

And I want you to know that the decision I have made has been mine and mine alone. This was a thing I

Wallis Simpson and the Duke of Windsor at the Château de Candé just before their wedding in June 1937.

had to judge entirely for myself. The other person most nearly concerned has tried up to the last to persuade me to take a different course. I have made this, the most serious decision of my life, only upon the single thought of what would in the end be best for all.

This decision has been made less difficult to me by the sure knowledge that my brother, with his long training in the public affairs of this country and with his fine qualities, will be able to take my place forthwith, without interruption or injury to the life and progress of the Empire. And he has one matchless blessing, enjoyed by so many of you and not bestowed on me – a happy home with his wife and children.

During these hard days I have been comforted by Her Majesty my mother and by my family. The Ministers of the Crown, and in particular Mr Baldwin, the Prime Minister, have always treated me with full consideration. There has never been any constitutional difference between me and them and between me and Parliament. Bred in the constitutional tradition by my father, I should never have allowed any such issue to arise.

Ever since I was Prince of Wales, and later on when I occupied the Throne, I have been treated with the greatest kindness by all classes of the people, wherever I have lived or journeyed throughout the Empire. For that I am very grateful.

I now quit altogether public affairs, and I lay down my burden. It may be some time before I return to my native land, but I shall always follow the fortunes of the British race and Empire with profound interest, and if at any time in the future I can be found of service to His Majesty in a private station I shall not fail.

And now we all have a new King. I wish him, and you, his people, happiness and prosperity with all my heart. God bless you all. God Save the King.

Duke of Windsor, 1936

Postscript

After he abdicated, Edward was given a new title, the Duke of Windsor, and married Mrs Simpson. However, he was forced to leave England for ever. He lived in exile in France until his death in 1972. His brother George took over the throne, becoming George VI. When he died in 1952, his daughter Elizabeth became Queen Elizabeth II.

7

World War II is declared

Neville Chamberlain, the British Prime Minister, made this radio broadcast – explaining that World War II had begun – on the morning of 3 September 1939.

I am speaking to you from the cabinet room at 10 Downing Street.

This morning the British Ambassador in Berlin handed the German Government a final note stating that, unless we heard from them by 11 o'clock that they were prepared at once to withdraw their troops from Poland, a state of war would exist between us.

I have to tell you now that no such undertaking has been received, and that consequently this country is at war with Germany.

You can imagine what a bitter blow it is to me that all my long struggle to win peace has failed. Yet I cannot believe that there is anything more or anything different that I could have done and that would have been more successful …

Now may God bless you all. May He defend the right. It is the evil things that we shall be fighting against – brute force, bad faith, injustice, oppression and persecution – and against them I am certain that the right will prevail.

Neville Chamberlain, 1939

Postscript

World War II, against Germany (led by Adolf Hitler) lasted for six years and drew in most of the countries of Europe, Russia, the United States and Japan. Germany and Japan were defeated in 1945.

8

The death of Gandhi

Mahatma Gandhi was the leader of the Indian National Congress, fighting against the British for a free India. He employed only peaceful methods such as marches, sit-downs and hunger strikes. Gandhi achieved his goal, but he was assassinated in 1948. The Prime Minister of India, Jawaharlal Nehru, announced his death on the radio.

Friends and comrades, the light has gone out of our lives and there is darkness everywhere. I do not know what to tell you and how to say it. Our beloved leader, Bapu as we called him, the father of the nation, is no more. Perhaps I am wrong to say that. Nevertheless, we will not see him again as we have seen him for these many years. We will not run to him for advice and seek solace from him, and that is a terrible blow, not to me only, but to millions and millions in this country, and it is a little difficult to soften the blow by any other advice that I or anyone else can give you.

The light has gone out, I said, and yet I was wrong. For the light that shone in this country was no ordinary light. The light that has illumined this country for these many years will illumine this country for many more years, and a thousand years later that light will still be seen in this country and the world will see it and it will give solace to innumerable hearts.

Jawaharlal Nehru, 1948

Photograph of Mahatma Gandhi giving a speech to crowds in 1935.

Postscript

Nehru, who gave this speech, died in 1964, but his daughter Indira Gandhi and his grandson Rajiv Gandhi both became Prime Minister of India after him, and both of them were killed by assassins. The family are still involved in Indian politics.

9

Ronald Reagan addresses the survivors of the Normandy Landings

On the 40th anniversary of the 1944 Normandy Landings, the soldiers who survived met by the graves near the beach to remember the many who had died. Ronald Reagan was the President of the United States.

We stand on a lonely, windswept point on the northern shore of France. The air is soft, but forty years ago at this moment, the air was dense with smoke and the cries of men, and the air was filled with the crack of rifle fire and the roar of cannon. At dawn, on the morning of the 6th of June 1944, 225 Rangers jumped off the British landing craft and ran to the bottom of these cliffs. Their mission was one of the most difficult and daring of the invasion: to climb these sheer and desolate cliffs and take out the enemy guns. The Allies had been told that some of the mightiest of these guns were here and they would be trained on the beaches to stop the Allied advance.

The Rangers looked up and saw the enemy soldiers – at the edge of the cliffs shooting down at them with machine-guns and throwing grenades. And the American Rangers began to climb. They shot rope ladders over the face of these cliffs and began to pull themselves up. When one Ranger fell, another would take his place. When one rope was cut, a Ranger would grab another and begin his climb again. They climbed, shot back, and held their footing. Soon, one by one, the Rangers pulled themselves over the top, and in seizing the firm land at the top of these cliffs, they began to seize back the continent of Europe.

Two hundred and twenty-five came here. After two days of fighting only ninety could still bear arms.

Behind me is a memorial that symbolizes the Ranger daggers that were thrust into the top of these cliffs. And before me are the men who put them there.

These are the boys of Pointe du Hoc. These are the men who took the cliffs. These are the champions who helped free a continent. These are the heroes who helped end a war.

Gentlemen, I look at you and I think of the words of Stephen Spender's poem.★ You are men who in your 'lives fought for life ... and left the vivid air signed with your honor'.

Forty summers have passed since the battle that you fought here. You were young the day you took these cliffs; some of you were hardly more than boys, with the deepest joys of life before you. Yet you risked everything here. Why? Why did you do it? What impelled you to put aside the instinct for self-preservation and risk your lives to take these cliffs? What inspired all the men of the armies that met here? We look at you, and somehow we know the answer. It was faith, and belief; it was loyalty and love.

★ Stephen Spender's poem: the lines are taken from a poem called *The Truly Great* by the English writer Stephen Spender in 1933:

> Near the snow, near the sun, in the highest fields
> See how these names are fêted by the waving grass
> And by the streamers of white cloud
> And whispers of wind in the listening sky.
> The names of those who in their lives fought for life
> Who wore at their hearts the fire's centre.
> Born of the sun they travelled a short while towards the sun,
> And left the vivid air signed with their honour.

The men of Normandy had faith that what they were doing was right, faith that they fought for all humanity, faith that a just God would grant them mercy on this beachhead or on the next. It was the deep knowledge – and pray God we have not lost it – that there is a profound moral difference between the use of force for liberation and the use of force for conquest. You were here to liberate, not to conquer, and so you and those others did not doubt your cause. And you were right not to doubt.

You all knew that some things are worth dying for. One's country is worth dying for, and democracy is worth dying for, because it's the most deeply honorable form of government ever devised by man. All of you loved liberty. All of you were willing to fight tyranny, and you knew the people of your countries were behind you.

Ronald Reagan, 1984

Postscript

In 1984 when this speech was made, the young soldiers who had survived the battle were already old. Each year, there are fewer and fewer of them, and soon this battle will fall out of living memory.

10

The *Challenger* space shuttle explodes

On 28 January 1986, the space shuttle Challenger *exploded shortly after takeoff, killing everyone on board. Their families were watching from the ground. Millions of viewers around the world saw the tragedy happen live on their television screens. The President of the United States went on television to express sorrow.*

For the families of the seven, we cannot bear, as you do, the full impact of this tragedy. But we feel the loss, and we're thinking about you so very much. Your loved ones were daring and brave, and they had that special grace, that special spirit that says, 'Give me a challenge and I'll meet it with joy.' They had a hunger to explore the universe and discover its truths. They wished to serve, and they did. They served all of us.

We've grown used to wonders in this century. It's hard to dazzle us. But for twenty-five years the United States space programme has been doing just that. We've grown used to the idea of space, and perhaps we forget that we've only just begun. We're still pioneers. They, the members of the *Challenger* crew, were pioneers.

And I want to say something to schoolchildren of America who were watching the live coverage of the shuttle's takeoff. I know it is hard to understand, but sometimes painful things like this happen. It's all part of the process of exploration and discovery. It's all part of taking a chance and expanding man's horizons. The future doesn't belong to the fainthearted; it belongs to the brave.

Ronald Reagan, 1986

Postscript

The space shuttle programme continued. New shuttles were built, and *Challenger* was replaced by a craft called *Endeavour*.

The Challenger space shuttle explodes 73 seconds after takeoff.

11

Nelson Mandela takes power

Nelson Mandela led the ANC (African National Congress) in its long struggle against apartheid in South Africa. He spent 26 years in jail for his beliefs, and was finally freed in 1990. Apartheid was abolished and elections were held. He made this speech in 1994, when he was elected President of South Africa.

I stand before you humbled by your courage, with a heart full of love for all of you. I regard it as the highest honour to lead the ANC at this moment in our new history, and that we have been chosen to lead our country into the new century.

I pledge to use all my strength and ability to live up to your expectations of me as well as of the ANC.

Tomorrow, the entire ANC leadership and I will be back at our desks. We are rolling up our sleeves to begin tackling the problems our country faces. We ask you all to join us – go back to your jobs in the morning. Let's get South Africa working.

For we must, together and without delay, begin to build a better life for all South Africans. This means creating jobs, building houses, providing education and bringing peace and security for all.

The calm and tolerant atmosphere that prevailed during the elections depicts the type of South Africa we can build. It set the tone for the future. We might have our differences, but we are one people with a common destiny in our rich variety of culture, race and tradition.

Nelson Mandela speaks to a crowded stadium in Soweto after his release
from prison, February 11, 1990.

People have voted for the party of their choice and we respect that. This is democracy.

I hold out a hand of friendship to the leaders of all parties and their members, and ask all of them to join us in working together to tackle the problems we face as a nation. An ANC government will serve all the people of South Africa, not just ANC members.

We also commend the security forces for the sterling work done. This has laid a solid foundation for a truly professional security force, committed to the service of the people and loyalty to the new constitution.

Now is the time for celebration, for South Africans to join together to celebrate the birth of democracy. I raise a glass to you all for working so hard to achieve what can only be called a small miracle. Let our celebrations be in keeping with the mood set in the elections, peaceful, respectful and disciplined, showing we are a people ready to assume the responsibilities of government.

I promise that I will do my best to be worthy of the faith and confidence you have placed in me and my organization, the African National Congress. Let us build the future together, and toast a better life for all South Africans.

Nelson Mandela, 1994

Postscript

Nelson Mandela was President of South Africa until he retired in 1999. He visited England in 2007 to unveil a statue of himself in Parliament Square in the centre of London.

War

Making the call to arms

12

Queen Elizabeth I rallies her troops

When Queen Elizabeth I executed her cousin, Mary Queen of Scots, in 1587, for plotting her murder, it sent shock waves through the Catholic world. Spain sent its mighty fleet, the Armada, to attack England. The English Navy had assembled at the docks in Tilbury, ready to do battle. Queen Elizabeth I went to the docks to raise their spirits before the battle.

I am come amongst you, as you see, at this time, not for my recreation and disport, but being resolved, in the midst and heat of the battle, to live and die amongst you all; to lay down for my God, and for my kingdom, and my people, my honour and my blood, even in the dust.

I know I have the body but of a weak and feeble woman; but I have the heart and stomach of a king, and of a king of England too, and think foul scorn that Parma or Spain, or any prince of Europe, should dare to invade the borders of my realm; to which rather than any dishonour shall grow by me, I myself will take up arms, I myself will be your general, judge, and rewarder of every one of your virtues in the field. I know already, for your forwardness you have deserved rewards and crowns; and We do assure you in the word of a prince,

Elizabeth I rallies her forces against the Spanish Armada with a speech at Tilbury in 1588.

they shall be duly paid you. In the mean time, my lieutenant general shall be in my stead, that whom never prince commanded a more noble or worthy subject; not doubting but by your obedience to my general, by your concord in the camp, and your valour in the field, we shall shortly have a famous victory over those enemies of my God, of my kingdom, and of my people.

Queen Elizabeth I, 1588

Postscript
The sea battle that followed this speech was one of the most famous in history. The British won.

13

A conscientious objector

In times of war, ordinary citizens are required to enter the army and fight for their country. Some people refuse to fight on principle, and they are called conscientious objectors. Philip Ford was called to appear before a court to explain why he had not joined the army as instructed in January 1679.

QUESTIONER: Complaint is made that you appeared not with your arms according to summons.
PHILIP FORD: Here's a summons dated the 7th of February last which I received.

QUESTIONER: Received you not one before?
FORD: Yes.

QUESTIONER: Wherefore did you not then appear?
FORD: Before the first summons came I received a summons from the Prince of Peace to march under his

banner, which is love, who came not to destroy men's lives but to save them. And being listed under this banner I dare not desert my colours to march under the banner – shop – of the kings of the earth.

Philip Ford, 1679

Postscript
The judge did not accept his argument. Philip Ford was fined £5 for each refusal to join the army. At the time, this was an enormous sum of money.

14

They will carry in their hearts the image

David Lloyd George made this speech in London to an audience of fellow Welsh people, urging them to support World War I.

May I tell you in a simple parable what I think this war is doing for us? I know a valley in North Wales, between the mountains and the sea. It is a beautiful valley, snug, comfortable, sheltered by the mountains from all the bitter blasts. But it is very enervating, and I remember how the boys were in the habit of climbing the hill above the village to have a glimpse of the great mountains in the distance, and to be stimulated and freshened by the breezes which came from the hilltops, and by the great spectacle of their grandeur.

We have been living in a sheltered valley for generations. We have been too comfortable and too indulgent – many, perhaps, too selfish – and the stern hand of fate has scourged us to an elevation where we can see the great everlasting things that matter for a nation – the great peaks we had forgotten, of Honour, Duty, Patriotism, and, clad in glittering white, the great pinnacle of Sacrifice pointing like a rugged finger to Heaven.

We shall descend into the valleys again; but as long as the men and women of this generation last, they will carry in their hearts the image of those great mountain peaks whose foundations are not shaken, though Europe rock and sway in the convulsions of a great war.

David Lloyd George, 1914

Postscript
The war lasted for four years. David Lloyd George became Prime Minister in 1916, two years after this speech, and halfway through the war, which England won.

15

This was our finest hour

Winston Churchill was the Prime Minister of England during World War II. His speeches are remembered for rais-ing morale and for their fighting spirit. It is inspiring to know that as a boy Churchill had a stutter and a lisp, which he overcame with help from speech therapists. This speech was made in the House of Commons.

Photograph of Winston Churchill in 1940.

What General Weygand called the Battle of France is over. I expect that the Battle of Britain is about to begin. Upon this battle depends the survival of Christian civilization. Upon it depends our own British life, and the long continuity of our institutions and our Empire. The whole fury and might of the enemy must very soon be turned on us.

Hitler knows that he will have to break us in this island or lose the war. If we can stand up to him, all Europe may be free and the life of the world may move forward into broad, sunlit uplands. But if we fail, then the whole world, including the United States, including all that we have known and cared for, will sink into the abyss of a new Dark Age made more sinister, and perhaps more protracted, by the lights of perverted science.

Let us therefore brace ourselves to our duties and so bear ourselves that, if the British Empire and its Commonwealth last for a thousand years, men will still say, 'This was their finest hour.'

Winston Churchill, 1940

Postscript

Hitler's armies tried desperately to conquer Britain. Huge air raids poured bombs over London and major cities. Submarines lurked in the waters around Britain and torpedoed British ships. The country was on alert ready for an invasion by land, which never came. Britain gained allies to fight the war. After much persuasion, the Americans, mentioned in this speech, joined the war and helped to turn the tide. The war ended in 1945 and Hitler was defeated. He committed suicide in an underground bunker in Berlin.

16

I will not attack until we are ready

Montgomery was the general in charge of the new Eighth Army, which fought World War II in the desert against Rommel's German troops. Things were not going well at the time he made the speech, and his job was to lift the morale of his troops and steel them for victory.

Now I understand that Rommel is expected to attack at any moment. Excellent. Let him attack.

I would sooner it didn't come for a week, just give me time to sort things out. If we have two weeks to prepare we will be sitting pretty; Rommel can attack as soon as he likes, after that, and I hope he does.

Meanwhile, we ourselves will start to plan a great offensive; it will be the beginning of a campaign which will hit Rommel and his Army for six right out of Africa.

But first we must create a reserve Corps, mobile and strong in armour, which we will train *out of the line*.[1] Rommel has always had such a force in his Africa Corps, which is never used to hold the line but which is always in reserve, available for striking blows. Therein has been his great strength. We will create such a Corps ourselves, a British Panzer Corps; it will consist of two armoured Divisions and one motorized Division; I gave orders yesterday for it to begin to form, back in the Delta.[2]

---

[1] **Out of the line:** away from the fighting
[2] **Delta:** the army had a base in the delta, that part of Egypt where the River Nile flows into the Mediterranean Sea

I have no intention of launching our great attack until we are completely ready; there will be pressure from many quarters to attack soon; *I will not attack until we are ready*, and you can rest assured on that point.

Meanwhile, if Rommel attacks while we are preparing, let him do so with pleasure; we will merely continue with our own preparations and *we* will attack when *we* are ready, and not before.

I want to tell you that I always work on the Chief of Staff system. I have nominated Brigadier de Guingand as Chief of Staff Eighth Army. I will issue orders through him. Whatever he says will be taken as coming from me and will be acted on *at once*. I understand there has been a great deal of 'bellyaching' out here. By bellyaching I mean inventing poor reasons for *not* doing what one has been told to do.

All this is to stop at once.

I will tolerate no bellyaching.

If anyone objects to doing what he is told, then he can get out of it: and at once. I want that made very clear right down through the Eighth Army.

I have little more to say just at present. And some of you may think it is quite enough and may wonder if I am mad.

I assure you I am quite sane.

I understand there are people who often think I am slightly mad; so often that I now regard it as rather a compliment.

All I have to say to that is that if I am slightly mad, there are a large number of people I could name who are raving lunatics!!

What I have done is to get over to you the 'atmosphere' in which we will now work and fight; you must see that that atmosphere permeates right through the

Eighth Army to the most junior private soldier. All the soldiers must know what is wanted; when they see it coming to pass there will be a surge of confidence throughout the Army.

I ask you to give me your confidence and to have faith that what I have said will come to pass.

General Bernard Montgomery, 1942

Postscript

Montgomery's troops went into battle a fortnight later and turned defeat into victory. They became known as the 'Desert Rats'. Montgomery went on

Lieutenant General Bernard Montgomery watches the beginning of the German retreat during the battle of El Alamein, November 1942.

to have a glittering career. Three years later, the Germans surrendered to him, and the war in northern Europe was over.

17

You are not all going to die

General Patton commanded the part of the American Army that was to take back France from the Germans towards the end of World War II. This was delivered the evening before they stormed the beaches of northern France on D-Day (6 June 1944). He didn't use any notes.

You are here today for three reasons. First, you are here to defend your homes and your loved ones. Second, you are here for your own self-respect, because you would not want to be anywhere else. Third, you are here because you are real men and all real men like to fight. When you, here, every one of you, were kids, you all admired the champion marble player, the fastest runner, the toughest boxer, the big league ball players, and the All-American football players. Americans love a winner. Americans will not tolerate a loser. Americans despise cowards. Americans play to win all of the time. I wouldn't give a hoot in hell for a man who lost and laughed. That's why Americans have never lost nor will ever lose a war; for the very idea of losing is hateful to an American.

You are not all going to die. Only two per cent of you right here today would die in a major battle. Death must not be feared. Death, in time, comes to all men. Yes, every man is scared in his first battle. If he says he's not, he's a liar. Some men are cowards but they fight the same as the brave men or they get the hell slammed out of them watching men fight who are just as scared as they are. The real hero is the man who fights even though he is scared. Some men get over their fright in a minute under fire. For some, it takes an hour. For some it takes days. But a real man will never let his fear of death overpower his honour, his sense of duty to his country and his innate manhood.

Battle is the most magnificent competition in which a human being can indulge. It brings out all that is best and removes all that is base. Americans pride themselves on being He Men and they ARE He Men. Remember that the enemy is just as frightened as you are, and probably more so. They are not supermen ...

All of the real heroes are not storybook combat fighters, either. Every single man in this army plays a vital role. Don't ever let up. Don't ever think that your job is unimportant. Every man has a job to do and he must do it. Every man is a vital link in the great chain. What if every truck driver suddenly decided that he didn't like the whine of those shells overhead, turned yellow, and jumped headlong into a ditch? The cowardly bastard could say, 'Hell, they won't miss me, just one man in thousands.' But, what if every man thought that way? Where in the hell would we be now? What would our country, our loved ones, our homes, even this world, be like? No, goddamnit, Americans don't think like that. Every man does his job. Every man serves the whole. Every department, every unit, is important in the vast scheme of this war ...

Sure, we want to go home. We want this war over with. The quickest way to get it over with is to go get

Film still from the opening scene on Omaha beach of Stephen Spielberg's
Saving Private Ryan.

the guys who started it. The quicker they are whipped,
the quicker we can go home. The shortest way home is
through Berlin and Tokyo. And when we get to Berlin, I
am personally going to shoot that paperhanging★
son-of-a-bitch Hitler. Just like I'd shoot a snake!

There is one great thing that you men will all be able
to say after this war is over and you are home once again.
You may be thankful that twenty years from now when
you are sitting by the fireplace with your grandson on
your knee and he asks you what you did in the great
World War II, you won't have to cough, shift him to the
other knee and say, 'Well, your granddaddy shovelled shit
in Louisiana.' No, sir, you can look him straight in the

★Paperhanging: Hitler in his early life had worked as a house decorator

37

eye and say, 'Son, your granddaddy rode with the great Third Army and a son-of-a-goddamned-bitch named Georgie Patton!'

General George Patton, 1944

Postscript
The next day, the English, Canadian, French and American armies stormed German-held beaches in northern France and came under heavy fire. The battle of Omaha beach is portrayed in the opening of the film *Saving Private Ryan*. However, they succeeded in their mission and won the war in the following year.

18

I cannot believe that this is to be the end

Bertrand Russell led the campaign against the nuclear arms race. He made this speech after the explosion of the first hydrogen bomb.

As geological time is reckoned, Man has so far existed for a very short period – one million years at the most. What he has achieved, especially during the last 6,000 years, is something utterly new in the history of the Cosmos, so far at least as we are acquainted with it.

For countless ages the sun rose and set, the moon waxed and waned, the stars shone in the night, but it was only with the coming of Man that these things were understood.

In the great world of astronomy and in the little world of the atom, Man has unveiled secrets which might have been thought undiscoverable. In art and literature and religion, some men have shown a sublimity of feeling which makes the species worth preserving.

Is all this to end in trivial horror because so few are able to think of Man rather than of this or that group of men? Is our race so destitute of wisdom, so incapable of impartial love, so blind even to the simplest dictates of self-preservation, that the last proof of its silly cleverness is to be the extermination of all life on our planet? – for it will be not only men who will perish, but also the animals, whom no one can accuse of communism or anti-communism.

I cannot believe that this is to be the end. I would have men forget their quarrels for a moment and reflect that, if they will allow themselves to survive, there is every reason to expect the triumphs of the future to exceed immeasurably the triumphs of the past.

There lies before us, if we choose, continual progress in happiness, knowledge, and wisdom. Shall we, instead, choose death, because we cannot forget our quarrels?

I appeal, as a human being to human beings: remember your humanity, and forget the rest. If you can do so, the way lies open to a new Paradise; if you cannot, nothing lies before you but universal death.

Bertrand Russell, 1954

Postscript

Bertrand Russell spent his life arguing against the development of nuclear weapons. Over the years there have been strong shows of feeling like large marches and camps such as that at Greenham Common. However, the development of nuclear weapons has continued. Eight countries are known to have used nuclear weapons in tests, and a handful more are thought to have them ready.

Justice

Demanding rights

19

Without the blush of shame and slavery upon his cheek

This speech was made at a chartist rally on Kensal Moor in 1838. The chartists were demanding better rights for ordinary working men, who at that time could not vote and lived in extreme poverty. In particular, they demanded the vote for all ('universal suffrage'). The speech was reported in their newspaper, the **Northern Star.**

Behind universal suffrage★ I want to see that knowledge in the mind, that principle in the heart, that power in the conscience, that strength in the right arm that would enable the working man to meet his master boldly, upright on his feet, without the brand mark of the bondman upon his brow, and without the blush of shame and slavery upon his cheek.

I want to see the working man as free in the mill as when he goes into the wilderness – as free spoken when he goes for his wages as he is when he spends a part of it with his companion.

I want to see every man so free as to speak his mind, act according to his conscience, and do no one any injury.

J. R. Stephens, 1838

★ **universal suffrage:** votes for all

Engraving of a Chartist meeting on Kennington Common, London.

Postscript

In the following year, the Chartists signed a petition calling on parliament to give the vote to all men, but parliament refused to accept the petition. Violence broke out, but the Chartists were not well organised and the movement died out a few years later. Votes for all were not achieved in England until 1928.

20

Ain't I a woman?

Sojourner Truth was a black American woman born into slavery and, having no education, she could not read or write. She had several children who were taken from her and sold. She was given her freedom when New York passed a law against slavery. She made powerful speeches in favour of rights for women, and often sang, too. She made this speech at a meeting about the rights of women in 1852. She spoke without notes; her words were captured by one of the audience.

That man over there say a woman needs to be helped into carriages and lifted over ditches and to have the best place everywhere. Nobody ever helped me into carriages or over mud puddles or gives me the best place … and ain't I a woman?

Look at me. Look at my arm! I have ploughed and planted and gathered into barns and no man could head me … and ain't I a woman?

I could work as much and eat as much as a man – when I could get to it – and bear the lash as well … and ain't I a woman?

I have borne 13 children and seen most all sold into slavery and when I cried out a mother's grief, none but Jesus heard me … and ain't I a woman?

That little man in black there say a woman can't have as much rights as a man 'cause Christ wasn't a woman. Where did your Christ come from? From God and a woman! Man had nothing to do with him!

If the first woman God ever made was strong enough to turn the world upside down all alone, together women ought to be able to turn it rightside up again!

Sojourner Truth, 1852

Postscript

Slavery was not abolished throughout America until 30 years after Sojourner Truth made this speech, and it was another 68 years before American women got the vote.

21

Return a verdict of not guilty!

Clarence Darrow rose to his feet on 19 May 1924 to defend Henry Sweet from a charge of murder. Henry Sweet had fired a shot into an angry mob that was attacking his brother's house in Chicago. It was a racist attack. The crowd was entirely white, and their purpose was to drive away Sweet's black family, who had moved into the neighbourhood. Terrified, he tried to disperse the crowd by firing a shot, but it killed a man.

We come now to lay this man's case in the hands of a jury of our peers — the first defence and the last defence is the protection of home and life as provided by our law. We are willing to leave it here. I feel, as I look at you, that we will be treated fairly and decently, even understandingly and kindly. You know what this case is. You know why it is. You know that if white men had been fighting their way against coloured men, nobody would ever have dreamed of a prosecution. And you know that from the beginning of this case to the end, up to the time you write your verdict, the prosecution is based on race prejudice and nothing else.

Gentlemen, I feel deeply on this subject; I cannot help it. Let us take a little glance at the history of the Negro race. It seems to me that the story would melt hearts of stone. I was born in America. I could have left it if I had wanted to go away. Some other men, reading about this land of freedom that we brag about on the Fourth of July, came voluntarily to America. These men, the defendants, are here because they could not help it. Their ancestors were captured in the jungles and on the plains of Africa, captured as you capture wild beasts, torn from their homes and their kindred; loaded into slave ships, packed like sardines in a box, half of them dying on the ocean passage; some jumping into the sea in their frenzy, when they had a chance to choose death in place of slavery. They were captured and brought here. They could not help it. They were bought and sold as slaves, to work without pay, because they were black. They were subject to all of this for generations, until finally they were given their liberty, so far as the law goes — and that is only a little way, because, after all, every human being's life in this world is inevitably mixed with every other life and, no matter what laws we pass, no matter what precautions we take, unless the people we meet are kindly and decent and human and liberty-loving, then there is no liberty. Freedom comes from human beings, rather than from laws and institutions.

Now, that is their history. These people are the children of slavery. If the race we belong to owes anything to any human being, or to any power in the universe, they owe it to these black men. Above all other men, they owe an obligation and a duty to these black men that can never be repaid. I never see one of them that I do not feel I ought to pay part of the debt of my race — and if you gentlemen feel as you should feel in this case, your emotions will be like mine.

Gentlemen, you are called into this case by chance. It took us a week to find you, a week of culling out prejudice and hatred. Probably we did not cull it all out at that; but we took the best and the fairest that we could find. It is up to you.

Your verdict means something in this case. It means something more than the fate of this boy. It is not often that a case is submitted to twelve men where the decision may mean a milestone in the history of the human race. But this case does. And I hope and I trust that you have a feeling of responsibility that will make you take it and do your duty as citizens of a great nation, and as members of the human family, which is better still. Let me say just a parting word for Henry Sweet, who has well-nigh been forgotten. I am serious, but it seems almost like a reflection upon this jury to talk as if I doubted your verdict. What has this boy done? This one boy now that I am culling out from all of the rest, and whose fate is in your hands – can you tell me what he has done? Can I believe myself? Am I standing in a court of justice where twelve men on their oaths are asked to take away the liberty of a boy twenty-one years of age, who has done nothing more than what Henry Sweet has done?

Gentlemen, you may think he shot too quick; you may think he erred in judgment; you may think that Dr Sweet should not have gone there prepared to defend his home. But, what of this case of Henry Sweet? What has he done? I want to put it up to you, each one of you, individually. Dr Sweet was his elder brother. He had helped Henry through school. He loved him. He had taken him into his home. Henry had lived with him and his wife; he had fondled his baby. The doctor had promised Henry the money to go through school. Henry was getting his education, to take his place in the world, gentlemen – and this is a hard job. With his brother's help he has worked his way through college up to the last year.

The doctor had bought a home. He feared danger. He moved in with his wife and he asked this boy to go with him. And this boy went to defend his brother, and his brother's wife and his child and his home.

Do you think more of him or less of him for that? I never saw twelve men in my life – and I have looked at a good many faces of a good many juries – I never saw twelve men in my life that, if you could get them to understand a human case, were not true and right.

Should this boy have gone along and helped his brother? Or, should he have stayed away? What would you have done? And yet, gentlemen, here is a boy, and the president of his college came all the way from Ohio to tell you what he thinks of him. His teachers have come here, from Ohio, to tell you what they think of him. The Methodist bishop has come here to tell you what he thinks of him.

So, gentlemen, I am justified in saying that this boy is as kindly, as well disposed, as decent a man as one of you twelve. Do you think he ought to be taken out of school and sent to the penitentiary? All right, gentlemen, if you think so, do it. It's your job, not mine. If you think so, do it. But if you do, gentlemen, if you should ever look into the face of your own boy, or your own brother, or look into your own heart, you will regret it in sackcloth and ashes*. You know, if he committed any offence, it was being loyal and true to his brother whom he loved. I know where you will send him and it will not be to a penitentiary.

I do not believe in the law of hate. I may not be true to my ideals always, but I believe in the law of love, and

---

*sackcloth and ashes: as a sign of remorse, a sinner would replace his clothes with sackcloth and cover his body with ashes to show that he truly repented of his sins

I believe you can do nothing with hatred. I would like to see a time when man loves his fellow man and forgets his color or his creed. We will never be civilized until that time comes. I know the Negro race has a long road to go. I believe that the life of the Negro race has been a life of tragedy, of injustice, of oppression. The law has made him equal, but man has not. And, after all, the last analysis is: what has man done? – and not what has the law done? I know there is a long road ahead of him before he can take the place which I believe he should take. I know that before him there is sorrow, tribulation, and death among the blacks, and perhaps the whites. I am sorry. I would do what I could to avert it. I would advise patience; I would advise tolerance; I would advise understanding; I would advise all those things which are necessary for men who live together.

Gentlemen, what do you think of your duty in this case? I have watched day after day these black, tense faces that have crowded this court. These black faces that now are looking to you twelve whites, feeling that the hopes and fears of a race are in your keeping.

This case is about to end, gentlemen. To them, it is life. Not one of their color sits on this jury. Their fate is in the hands of twelve whites. Their eyes are fixed on you, their hearts go out to you, and their hopes hang on your verdict.

This is all. I ask you, on behalf of this defendant, on behalf of these helpless ones who turn to you, and more than that – on behalf of this great state, and this great city, which must face this problem and face it fairly – I ask you in the name of progress and of the human race, to return a verdict of not guilty in this case!

Clarence Darrow, 1924

Postscript
The jury found Sweet innocent and he went free.

22

The whole system's wrong

The following speech is a transcript from a BBC radio programme about unemployment in which jobless workers spoke about their experiences.

The whole system's wrong, and I don't think you'll ever change the hearts of these industrialists unless something very drastic is done. All they want is to get everything out of you, to the last possible ounce.

One employer said to me, 'From a business point of view you're less valuable to me than a drum of oil. We must have the oil, but we can do without you.' This is the

Picture of unemployed demonstrators in Sheffield, from the *Sheffield Daily Independent,* 8th October 1931.

type of man responsible for the system – people working ten and twelve hours a day, sweated half to death on the point-to-point and other speeding-up-production methods.

All the time the development of machinery is simplifying skill and doing away with us older fellows. It affects men over twenty – yes, it's come down to twenty now. Many employers today favour women and juveniles, who when they become entitled to a higher scale of wages find themselves on the scrapheap with the others. I'm only thirty-three, but I've been told time after time that I'm too old, and some of my friends who are over forty know for a fact that they'll never get another job whilst we live under this present system.

There's plenty of gold, plenty of material, and God knows there's plenty of labour, so what's wrong? I'm not a revolutionary in the sense of violence, but we do want a revolutionary change in our conditions and unless this change comes quick, thousands like myself are condemned to live in despair and slow starvation, watching our wives and children rot before our eyes.

Neither Fascism nor Communism nor any other 'ism' holds any terror for us. *Nothing* can be worse than what we've got at present.

John Evans, 1934

Postscript

The growth of communism and fascism in other countries was watched carefully by all parts of English society. Many people thought that one of these two great social movements might take root in England. It did not happen. However, the Labour Party, which was still young at the time of this speech, did grow, and attracted the support of working people who wanted a say in the way the country was managed.

The American Dream

Speeches by Americans

23

The Gettysburg Address

This famous short speech was made by Abraham Lincoln when he was President of the United States. A civil war was raging between the north and south of the country, and a great battle had just taken place at Gettysburg, in which many men died. Lincoln spoke at a ceremony in the graveyard.

Four score and seven years ago our fathers brought forth on this continent a new nation, conceived in liberty and dedicated to the proposition that all men are created equal. Now we are engaged in a great civil war, testing whether that nation or any nation so conceived and so dedicated can long endure. We are met on a great battle-field of that war.

We have come to dedicate a portion of that field as a final resting-place for those who here gave their lives that that nation might live. It is altogether fitting and proper that we should do this.

But in a larger sense, we cannot dedicate, we cannot consecrate, we cannot hallow this ground. The brave men, living and dead who struggled here have consecrated it far above our poor power to add or detract. The world will little note nor long remember what we say here, but it can never forget what they did here.

Illustration of Abraham Lincoln giving his Gettysburg Address. No known photographs exist of the actual speech.

It is for us the living rather to be dedicated here to the unfinished work which they who fought here have thus far nobly advanced. It is rather for us to be here dedicated to the great task remaining before us – that from these honoured dead we take increased devotion to that cause for which they gave the last full measure of devotion – that we here highly resolve that these dead shall not have died in vain, that this nation under God shall have a new birth of freedom, and that government of the people, by the people, for the people shall not perish from the earth.

Abraham Lincoln, 1863

Postscript

The battle at Gettysburg turned out to be the turning point of the American Civil War, which the North won. Slavery was abolished. Lincoln was assassinated two years later by John Wilkes Booth. Today, his words are engraved on the wall of the Lincoln Memorial in Washington.

24

The Cold War

Eisenhower was the President of the United States at a time when the Soviet Union was growing in power. As the two superpowers raced to build their nuclear store of weapons, there was worldwide fear that they would go to war, and that this war would destroy the entire world. Eisenhower needed to reassure the American people, but he also had to sound strong to the Soviet Union.

The worst to be feared and the best to be expected can be simply stated.

The *worst* is atomic war.

The *best* would be this: a life of perpetual fear and tension; a burden of arms draining the wealth and labour of all peoples; a wasting of strength that defies the American system or the Soviet system or any system to achieve true abundance and happiness for the peoples of this earth.

Every gun that is made, every warship launched, every rocket fired signifies, in the final sense, a theft from those who hunger and are not fed, those who are cold and are not clothed.

This world in arms is not spending money alone.

It is spending the sweat of its labourers, the genius of its scientists, the hopes of its children.

The cost of one heavy bomber is this: a modern brick school in more than thirty cities.

It is two electric power plants, each serving a town of 60,000 population.

It is two fine, fully equipped hospitals.

It is some fifty miles of concrete highway.

We pay for a single fighter plane with a half million bushels of wheat.

We pay for a single destroyer with new homes that could have housed more than 8,000 people.

This, I repeat, is the best way of life to be found on the road the world has been taking.

This is not a way of life at all, in any true sense. Under the cloud of threatening war, it is humanity hanging from a cross of iron.

Dwight D. Eisenhower, 1953

Postscript

The nuclear arms race continued. Russia and America came close to conflict during the so-called 'Cold War' when the relationship between them was jumpy and suspicious. But Eisenhower remained popular. In fact, he was re-elected as President three years later. But the tension between the countries continued until the end of communism in the Soviet Union in the 1980s.

25

We will choose life

Lyndon B. Johnson became President of the United States when it was fighting an unpopular war in Vietnam. Hundreds of American soldiers had died and little progress had been made. Under a lot of pressure to withdraw, Johnson made this speech offering to open negotiations about its future.

We often say how impressive power is. But I do not find it impressive at all. The guns and the bombs, the rockets and the warships, are all symbols of human failure. They are necessary symbols. They protect what we cherish. But they are witness to human folly.

A dam built across a great river is impressive.

In the countryside where I was born, and where I live, I have seen the night illuminated, and the kitchens warmed, and the homes heated, where once the cheer-less night and the ceaseless cold held sway. And all this happened because electricity came to our area along the humming wires of the REA*. Electrification of the countryside – yes, that too, is impressive.

A rich harvest in a hungry land is impressive.

The sight of healthy children in a classroom is impressive.

These – not mighty arms – are the achievements which the American Nation believes to be impressive.

And, if we are steadfast, the time may come when all other nations will also find it so.

Every night before I turn out the lights to sleep I ask myself this question: Have I done everything that I can do to unite this country? Have I done everything I can to help unite the world, to try to bring peace and hope to all the peoples of the world? Have I done enough?

Ask yourselves that question in your homes – and in this hall tonight. Have we, each of us, all done all we could? Have we done enough?

★REA: Rural Electric Association

We may well be living in the time foretold many years ago when it was said: 'I call heaven and earth to record this day against you, that I have set before you life and death, blessing and cursing: therefore choose life, that both thou and thy seed may live.'

This generation of the world must choose: destroy or build, kill or aid, hate or understand.

We can do all these things on a scale never dreamed of before.

Well, we will choose life.

Lyndon B. Johnson, 1965

Postscript

America did not withdraw its troops from Vietnam until 1975, and the communist North won the war. In all, the war lasted 15 years and one and a half million people died in it.

American soldiers carry a wounded colleague from the jungle in Tay Ninh, South Vietnam, in April 1967.

26

The American dream

This was a speech made by Richard Nixon during his campaign to become the President of the United States.

Tonight, I see the face of a child. He lives in a great city, he's black or he's white, he's Mexican, Italian, Polish, none of that matters. What matters: he's an American child.

That child in that great city is more important than any politician's promise. He is America, he is a poet, he is a scientist, he's a great teacher, he's a proud craftsman, he's everything we've ever hoped to be in everything we dare to dream about.

He sleeps the sleep of a child, and he dreams the dreams of a child. And yet when he awakens, he awakens to a living nightmare of poverty, neglect and despair.

He fails in school, he ends up on welfare. For him the American system is one that feeds his stomach and starves his soul. It breaks his heart. And in the end it may take his life on some distant battlefield.

To millions of children in this rich land this is their prospect, but this is only part of what I see in America.

I see another child tonight. He hears a train go by. At night he dreams of faraway places where he'd like to go. It seems like an impossible dream. But he is helped on his journey through life. A father who had to go to work before he finished the sixth grade sacrificed everything he had so that his sons could go to college.

A gentle Quaker mother with a passionate concern for peace quietly wept when he went to war but she understood why he had to go.

Photograph of Richard Nixon speaking in Santa Barbara during the 1968 American Presidential campaign.

A great teacher, a remarkable football coach, an inspirational minister encouraged him on his way. A courageous wife and loyal children stood by him in victory and also in defeat.

And in his chosen profession of politics, first there were scores, then hundreds, then thousands, and finally millions who worked for his success.

And tonight he stands before you, nominated for President of the United States of America.

You can see why I believe so deeply in the American dream.

For most of us the American revolution has been won, the American dream has come true. What I ask of you tonight is to help me make that dream come true for millions to whom it's an impossible dream today.

Richard Nixon, 1968

Postscript

Nixon won the campaign and became the President of the United States. He is more often remembered for the way he left office in disgrace in 1974, after the Watergate Scandal.

The Publishers would like to thank the following for permission to reproduce copyright material:

Photo credits

p.2 © Hulton–Deutsch Collection/Corbis; **p.7** © Bettmann/Corbis; **p.12** © Bettmann/Corbis; **p.16** Hulton Archive/Getty Images; **p.21** © Bettmann/Corbis; **p.23** © Peter Turnley/Corbis; **p.26** Private Collection/© Look and Learn/The Bridgeman Art Library; **p.30** H. F. Davis/Topical Press Agency/Getty Images; **p.34** © Imperial War Museum, image E 18980; **p.37** © Corbis SYGMA; **p.42** Mary Evans Picture Library/Alamy; **p.49** Image S03742 from the collections in Sheffield local Studies Library, reproduced with kind permission; **p.54** © Bettmann/Corbis; **p.58** © Bettmann/Corbis; **p.60** © Bettmann/Corbis

Acknowledgements

pp.38–40 extract from 'Shall we choose death?', BBC Radio, London, 30 December 1954. Reprinted by permission of The Bertrand Russell Peace Foundation Ltd. **pp.44–48** extract from 'The life of the Negro race has been a life of tragedy', Detroit, 19 May 1926, transcript published by the National Association for the Advancement of Colored People (NAACP), in 1927; **pp.49–50** extract from the *Time To Spare* BBC Radio series, 5 May 1934, reprinted in *The* Listener, 9 May 1934.

Every effort has been made to trace all copyright holders, but if any have been inadvertently overlooked the Publishers will be pleased to make the necessary arrangements at the first opportunity.